MEIRIONNYDD'S STORY

The History of Southern Gwynedd

by Michael Senior

ISBN: 0-86381-442-5

First published in 1997 by Gwasg Carreg Gwalch,
12 Iard yr Orsaf, Llanrwst, Wales LL26 0EH
☎ *(01492) 642031*
Printed and published in Wales.

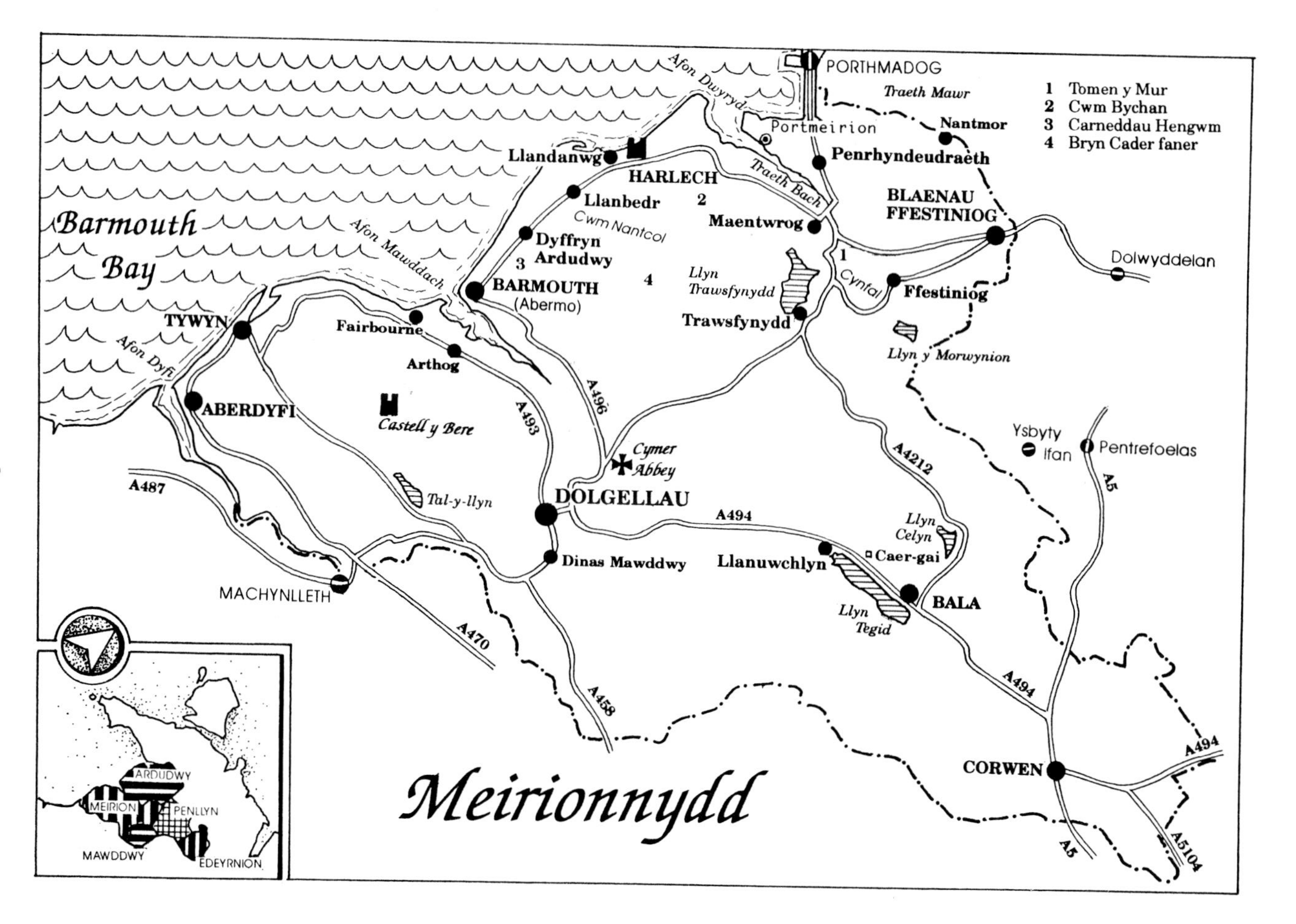
PORTHMADOG
Traeth Mawr
1 Tomen y Mur
2 Cwm Bychan
3 Carneddau Hengwm
4 Bryn Cader faner
Afon Dwyryd
Portmeirion
Nantmor
Penrhyndeudraeth
Llandanwg
HARLECH
Traeth Bach
BLAENAU FFESTINIOG
Llanbedr
2
Cwm Nantcol
Maentwrog
Barmouth Bay
Afon Mawddach
Dyffryn Ardudwy
3
4
Llyn Trawsfynydd
1
Cynfal
Ffestiniog
Dolwyddelan
BARMOUTH
(Abermo)
Trawsfynydd
TYWYN
Fairbourne
Arthog
Llyn y Morwynion
Afon Dyfi
ABERDYFI
Castell y Bere
A493
A496
Ysbyty Ifan
Pentrefoelas
Cymer Abbey
A4212
A5
A487
Tal-y-llyn
DOLGELLAU
A494
Llyn Celyn
Caer-gai
Dinas Mawddwy
Llanuwchlyn
MACHYNLLETH
BALA
Llyn Tegid
A470
A458
A494
CORWEN
A494
Meirionnydd
A5
A5104
ARDUDWY
MEIRION
PENLLYN
MAWDDWY
EDEYRNION

Introduction

Local government units have undergone several confusing changes since Edward I imposed on the old kingdom of Gwynedd the English county system. Under that system (now the one before last) Merionethshire was a county in its own right, and met Caernarfonshire at the Ffestiniog valley – the boundary, that is, between the two parts of the new Gwynedd dealt with in this and the companion booklet, 'Llŷn – The Peninsula's Story'.

That county, which had survived from the thirteenth century and so still gives the area an identity, was made up of three older units, the Welsh medieval divisions of Ardudwy (in the north), Penllyn inland, and Meirionnydd itself in the south. Although these three have much in common, lying as they do like a solid block of southern Gwynedd fronting Powys, there is no term which conveniently covers them all, and it must be said that the title of this booklet should correctly include them all. Because, however, all were incorporated for so long into the former county, the Welsh name of which is Meirionnydd, which (in a more recent manifestation) became a district council, it is that name which most naturally covers the area.

As an area its features are strong and mostly natural. It has North Wales's largest lakes, and broad areas of uninhabited upland terrain. Indeed it would be notable for being empty were it not for the fact that it contains a handful of towns of exceptional character, among which Dolgellau would stand out for its distinctiveness in even a more populated area. This area as a whole is in fact a place of old settlements, and its depths of history is accordingly unparalleled.

(1) Sarn Badrig, a straight bank of stones 13-14 miles long, thought by some to be the remains of Cantre'r Gwaelod's dykes

LAND AND WATER

JUST as the history of northern Gwynedd opened with a myth of a lost land so the ancient past of southern Gwynedd too is supposed to lie under the sea. Slightly nearer to history than that tale of the wizard Gwydion is the story of Cantre'r Gwaelod, which tells of events which are supposed to have taken place in the sixth century, the period of small kingdoms which followed the Roman withdrawal. The story itself is of considerable antiquity.

At that time, it says, the area off the coast between Harlech and Barmouth, now part of Cardigan Bay, was a rich and fertile land. Being lowlying (the name means 'Bottom hundred') it needed constant defence against the sea, and the story relates that one night the man in charge of the floodgates, being drunk, neglected to close them. The idyllic kingdom went under the waves.

The supposed corroboration is visible off the coast midway between Harlech and Barmouth. It is a bank of stones called Sarn Badrig (1) which starts from a point about a mile offshore and runs southwestwards for thirteen to fourteen miles. During the great period of coastal shipping in the last century it was notorious as a navigational hazard. Its name, translated as St Patrick's causeway, carries a further legend that it was the means which the saint used to cross between Ireland and Wales. The name 'Badrig' provides an alternative derivation, which may be only word-play, since it could be interpreted as 'boat-ripper'.

What makes this reef remarkable, and obliges us to consider the theory that it is manmade, is that for all its considerable length it is almost exactly straight. There are other such banks in the sea in this area, but none so dramatic as Sarn Badrig. Whether natural or not, they certainly indicate that there was dry land once where there is now sea.

There is no doubt that the coastline is constantly changing, and that both land and sea have risen and sunk at various times. Under the sand at many spots around our coast, and in some places exposed at low tide on the shore, there are fossilised forests. Illustrating graphically the change since Iron Age times, half the ring fort of Dinas Dinlle, in north-west Gwynedd, once forming a promontory, has now gone into the sea (2). Indeed the change is faster than that in places. The church at Llandanwg not far from Sarn Badrig, gets periodicaly immersed in sand. The exchange between land and water is, moreover, a two-way one. A plain now stretches for some three-quarters of a mile seawards from what was once the watergate of Harlech castle – though in this case, as we shall see, the situation is complicated by

(2) Dinas Dinlle, a coastal ring-fort becoming eroded by the sea

(3) The rock of Harlech

the change in course of a river. The rock of Harlech (clearly a place of importance long before Edward I built his fine fortress there) (3) is described in the Mabinogion story of 'Branwen' as "overlooking the sea", and clearly that feature would have added to its strategic usefulness.

The mention of Harlech in the story of Branwen is further evidence of the religious significance of this area in early times, since it specifies that it was a court of Brân, a personage who, behind the humanised character of the tale, is recognisable as an ancient European god, perhaps a river deity. Brân it was who owned the cauldron of rebirth, which was one of the early versions of the magic vessel which developed into the Holy Grail.

The story tells how those of Brân's followers who survived the final battle between the British and the Irish fled southwards with his severed head, evidently a magical talisman, and paused on the rock of Harlech for a feast which lasted seven years. The presence of the head counteracted the effect of the passage of time.

The area, in fact, is exceptionally rich in magical and mystical associations, all specifically located. The wizard Gwydion, who brought his protegé Lleu Llaw Gyffes to Caer Arianrhod, in the Llŷn area of north-west Gwynedd, had previously defeated Pryderi, the king of South Wales, by magic, on the sands of the Glaslyn estuary below Maentwrog. The fallen king was buried there, and the story particularly mentions his grave. There is indeed a prehistoric stone set into the wall of the church at Maentwrog (4), (itself perhaps built there because of the spot's prior sacredness), which reminds one of those sometimes to be found in burial chambers, a rounded monolith known as Twrog's stone.

The sequel of the story of Gwydion and Llew, as told in 'Math, son of Mathonwy', is specific to this area also, since the young hero set up court at Tomen y Mur, a Roman camp with an impressive and mysterious mound, which overlooks the lake of Trawsfynydd, at the very edge of the moorland (5). There his unfaithful wife Blodeuwedd tricked him into revealing how he might be slain, and her lover killed him on the bank of the river Cynfal. This tumbling stream flows strongly down its valley still, crossed by the road on which one ascends from Ffestiniog to Trawsfynydd. It was on that river also that Lleu, resurrected by Gwydion's magic, took his revenge (6). Magnanimously he allowed his rival to protect himself with a stone, but Lleu's spear passed through both the stone and the lover. "And there the stone is, on the bank of the Cynfael river in Ardudwy, and the hole through it." Remarkably there still exists there such a stone, though not on the bank

(4) Twrog's stone, Maentwrog church

(5) Tomen y Mur

of the Cynfal so much as on a slope above its valley. Indeed it was probably the occurrence of this odd feature that gave rise to this element of the tale.

His fickle wife Blodeuwedd was turned by Gwydion into an owl, and in that form bemoans her fate to this day, while her maidens fled from the court at Tomen y Mur on Gwydion's approach, and, looking backwards in fear, walked into the moorland lake above Ffestiniog and drowned, giving it the name it still bears, Llyn y Morwynion, 'the maidens' lake' (7).

The story of the inundation of Cantre'r Gwaelod has a sequel too, which tells how Elffin, the prince who had thus lost his inheritance, fished a weir on the river Dovey, south of our present area, where he found an abandoned child, who turned out to be the inspired bard Taliesin.

Taliesin and Gwydion are perhaps the two most powerful figures in the original native British mythology, and for them both to have associations with this area would in itself mark it out as being of special mystical importance, even if this coincidence were not reinforced by such a wealth of other material. Even inland, away from the coastal conflict of land and water, the theme of mysteries and inundations reccurs. Up at Bala the lake is, in fact, so large as to seem like an inland sea.

Legends abound here too, occurring in an atmosphere which is in any case rather otherwordly, affected as it is by elements such as those sudden mists which the lake produces sometimes from its surface, and the general dominance of natural forces, wind and water, hillside and cloud (8). Perhaps these old traditions find a remote descendant in the fervent outbreaks of religious commitment which, as we shall see, are part of the character of Bala, this area's sole (and remote) contact with the familiar reality of urban life. A notable modern descendant or survivor from more mysterious times is the lake's monster, which has been sighted several times in recent years and at present remains unexplained. The surface of that great sheet of water has always, it seems, suggested mysteries.

Though Bala town now is a fairly humble place there was a great city once (the legend says) beneath what is now the lake. The excesses of a wicked king brought about its downfall, and this submergence gives us the fine sheet of water we enjoy today. This is a common and universal folk-tale, the drowned luxurious land, perhaps reflecting partly real memories (since the flooded area has spread in early and pre-historic times over a once-dry alluvial valley) and partly possibly offering a symbol for our sense of a lost past when life was better than it now is.

This is the stuff of folk-tale, but there are more basic associations in myth

(6) The river Cynfal

(6) The stone with the hole, above the Cynfal valley

(7) Llyn Morwynion

in this area. Another remarkable tale connected with Bala manages to combine the mystical figure of Taliesin with an early form of that magic vessel which came from such diverse origins to become the Holy Grail, the mystical life-giving symbol sought by knights in medieval stories. One of its sites of origin in fact is an island on Bala lake, or Llyn Tegid, to give it is proper name, the 'beautiful lake'.

There lived on this island in mythical times a man called Tegid Foel and his wife Ceridwen, who had two children, Creirwy, the most beautiful girl in the world, and Afagddu, the ugliest boy. In order to compensate the latter for his ugliness Ceridwen decided to make him all-knowing. To do so she set about boiling a cauldron of knowledge and inspiration, the recipe for which she had in an ancient book. Casting into it the appropriate herbs at the right state of the stars, she set in motion one of the most appealing Welsh tales. Doing so she forms for us the pivotal point at which the Celtic sacred vessel which archeology indicates was a widespread and important religious form emerges from its silent past to generate its multiple offspring, life-giving or inspiring vessels still with us today in the form of the Christian chalice and the witch's cauldron.

The cauldron with which Ceridwen has accidentally inspired so many people ironically failed in its purpose of compensating her ugly son. One of the specifications was that it had to boil continuously for a year and a day, when it would yield the reduced potion of three drops of distilled inspiration. Ceridwen therefore put a boy, little Gwion, to stir it. Towards the end of the year, however, the three drops flew out of the cauldron and landed on Gwion's finger. Because they were hot he put his finger in his mouth, and instantly knew everything. Among the things he knew was that Ceridwen would try to destroy him.

There then began a succession of shape-changes which could be taken to refer to the Celtic belief in metampsychosis, the return of the soul in a different body after death. He changes into a hare, she, as a greyhound, pursues him; he sees a river and becomes a fish, but she is after him still as an otter; in the end he hides as a grain of wheat in a barn, but destiny is not so easily avoided. Ceridwen comes scratching among the wheat as a black hen, and swallows him.

Nine months later Gwion is again reborn, and after further fateful events takes up a new life as the inspired prophet Taliesin. The story says, in effect, that the wisdom of the poet Taliesin came from a former life in which he drank of the cauldron of inspiration possessed by the witch-goddess

(8) Bala lake

Ceridwen.

The evidence in the world of ideas for this area's early religious significance is supported also by substantial remains in the world of stone.

EARLY INHABITANTS

IF places like Ardudwy and Meirionnydd seem to us remote now, it is because we are adjusted to thinking of the basic means of travel as being across land. In those circumstances they are certainly cut off from the great world, by the very physical obstacle of a major mountain range. Quite the reverse, however, has been from time to time the case, and particularly in the early phases of man's civilisation the primary mode of transport was by sea. Viewed in the light of that, these mild coastal areas lie at a prime spot on a major seaway. Much of their prehistory may be explained at once by that simple fact.

One such feature which would otherwise be puzzling is the density of population from Neolithic, through Bronze Age and Iron Age times, which the prehistoric remains in this area clearly imply. Among the earliest monuments in Britain are the various styles of chambered tombs, and there are no less than six of these within a five-mile radius in the area of Harlech. Similarly the centre of the Llŷn peninsula boasts, as we may see in the companion booklet which tells its story, an equivalent number of Iron Age forts.

The chambered tombs, dating from about 2,500 B.C., are of a type which indicates connections with Ireland and southern Britain, particularly the Cotswold area, and it makes much sense to see this as a stopping point (based perhaps on the natural harbour formed by the mouth of the Artro river, near Llandanwg) between these two major Neolithic centres. The tombs here are of the 'portal' type, best examined perhaps in the two very fine examples which lie behind the school at Dyffryn Ardudwy (9).

Now two separate chambers, these are still surrounded by the remains of the vast mound of stones which originally united them in a single monument. The form, once one looks for it, is clear. A pair of uprights slightly higher than the others forms what appears to be a doorway at the eastern end of the chamber, their flat sides facing each other; a universal characteristic of this feature is that the apparent doorway is then blocked, in a way which must have been permanent and intrinsic to the design, by a slightly lower stone set across the gap between them to form the cross-piece, on a plan, of the letter H. Since this feature means that the portal cannot have been used as such, its nature must be symbolic or conventional. A result of the greater height of the portal stones is that the capstone slopes downwards slightly towards the west.

The capstones are normally smooth and flat underneath, but rounded and rough on top, suggesting perhaps that their underside was intended to be

(9) Cromlechs at Dyffryn Ardudwy

(10) Hengwm cairns

seen, by people entering the tomb, but that their exterior would have been covered. Indeed the tombs were always intended to be built over by a mound of stones, and the extent of such a covering can be seen in the Dyffryn example. The great field enclosures of the 19th century led to an enormous amount of wall-building, as may be plainly seen on the slopes and foothills around, and we know by comparing 18th-century descriptions and drawings with what may now be seen that a large quantity of the covering stones has in most instances been removed.

The tombs had in any case been robbed and damaged at earlier dates, and not much of interest has ever been found within them. When the Dyffryn chambers were investigated archeologically in 1962-3 some small pieces of Neolithic pottery were found, which helped to date the structure and indicate its phases of development. The cairns and chambers of the Carneddau Hengwm complex, a little to the south, have similarly been much damaged, but it remains impressive for its size and its situation (10).

Those mentioned here are by no means the only chambered tombs or cairns in our area, simply the best examples. There are fine ones too in northern Gwynedd at Cefnamlwch and in the area of Rhiw on the Llŷn peninsula; and, here in the southern area remnants of another chambered cairn at Cors y Gedol, the ancient house near Dyffryn which was the home of the Vaughan family.

A small piece of evidence that perhaps at one time more was to be seen at sacred sites such as these lies behind a pew at the back of the nearby church of St Peter at Llanbedr (11). It is a modest piece of stone, but it bears an image which connects it with the great burial mounds of the Boyne valley in Ireland and with many other ancient sites in Europe, the incised spiral figure which may well represent the endless cycles of decay and renewal.

The foothills and the range which blocks the hinterland of the Harlech coast from the Trawsfynydd valley are seamed with trackways. From the frequency along those of cairns and standing stones it seems that they must have been there at least as early as the Bronze Age. The well-known 'Roman Steps' (12), above Cwm Bychan, no doubt lie on such a route, ascending as they do to the natural pass of Bwlch Tyddiad. The steps themselves probably owe their origin not to the Romans but to the use of this way as a pack-horse track in the Middle Ages, and probably before.

A quite remarkable area, probably associated with a prehistoric trackway, lies above Llandecwyn, to the north of Harlech, in a valley rising to a point called Bryn Cader Faner, where a striking cairn is sited on a prominent knoll.

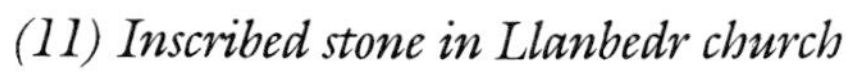

(11) Inscribed stone in Llanbedr church

(12) The 'Roman' steps

EARLY INHABITANTS

Here the whole land has a deep feeling of undisturbed ancientness. The ground is littered with signs of prehistoric works, cairns, circles, banks, walls, some clustered, some magnificently alone, many (neatly built and yet not prominently placed) defying explanation.

The traditional view of the change from one culture to another, which is visible to us from the style of the remains, sees the arrival of new people in the form of invasion. Although no doubt such events occurred, it may be too simple a way of explaining change, and possibly we should also imagine the continuous spreading, like a tide creeping up the beach, of new influences, new discoveries, innovations of technique. In any case the development of the use of metal tools enabled an advance from the early farming culture of the late stone age into a more settled and structured period which we know (for this reason) as the Bronze Age.

THE NEW ERA

THE Roman Empire relied largely on land transport, their chief weapon being their powerful network of roads. Along these armies could march at speed and messages be relayed. In spite of the difficulties they penetrated North Wales as far as Caernarfon, formed a camp at the edge of the moor above Trawsfynydd (5, 13) and another, quite recently discovered, at Dolbenmaen at the peninsula's neck; but they did not apparently attempt to colonise Llŷn, and their presence is mainly transitory in the foothills of Ardudwy.

The camp at Dolbenmaen may have been a posting point on the route between the major fort of Segontium at Caernarfon, and the auxiliary outpost at Tomen y Mur. The latter (mentioned already in connection with the Mabinogion story in which it was the seat of the hero Lleu Llaw Gyffes) is of some importance, since it was the point at which the road from Segontium and that from Canovium in the Conwy Valley joined up on their route southwards to the South Wales centre Moridunum, now Carmarthen.

At Tomen y Mur there are extensive remains to be seen, now mainly in the form of grass banks, including the area of an amphitheatre, a little way from the main fort. The most conspicuous feature is the mound or 'tomen' which gives the place its name, thought to be the motte of a medieval castle, which would have been a wooden structure on its top, probably built by an English earl attempting invasion. The most striking quality of the site is its extreme exposure, a bleakness and lack of shelter which must have tested the hardiness of its Roman garrison.

This neat network of roads is further linked to the overall British structure by a southerly spur from Chester, protected by a small fort at the head of Llyn Tegid, before it comes down the valley to join the main road at Dolgellau.

Caer Gai, as the fort is called, lies on a hillside overlooking the valley of the Dyfrdwy and the present road, unusually elevated for a Roman fort (14). In early tradition the name is associated with a figure of British myth, none other than King Arthur's foster-brother Cai, later known as Sir Kay. The Elizabethan poet Spenser, evidently having heard of this tradition, places King Arthur's fosterage in this upper valley of the Dee in his epic 'The Fairy Queen'. From equally early times, however, it was also recognised that Caer Gai was Roman, and Pennant notes that "multitudes of coins have been found in different parts of the neighbourhood". His predecessor Camden, in the 16th century, ascribed the name to a Roman leader Caius, and this may well reflect an accurate record.

(13) Tomen y Mur, site of a Roman camp

(14) Caer Gai, a Roman fort near Bala

(14) The base of the rampart of the Roman fort of Caer Gai now forms part of a modern enclosure

Roman it indoubtedly is, whether or not before that (as its hilltop position suggests) a British fort. The wall which is visible from the road is probably part of the Roman fort but improved to its present form to make a retaining wall lining the Roman rampart. This forms a flat terraced area inside the fort, probably a lanscaping feature connected with the Tudor manor house which stands at the centre of the fort. This latter was a seat of the Vaughan family, as indeed were several of the larger houses of this area.

There are signs that the Roman road towards Chester set off from the north-east side of the fort, near where the entrance to the farmyard now is. An inscribed stone found in the field on this side indicated that the fort was garrisoned in the early second century A.D. by the First Cohort of Nervii, and other artefacts, burial urns and coins found in a nearby field, indicate occupation at the end of the first century; but we do not know any more about the history of Caer Gai than these slight clues tell us, or than we can guess from its commanding position at the end of the valley with an outlook over a wide stretch of the river.

Beyond the other end of the lake, above the probable line of the Roman road and the present main road lay a substantial Iron Age fort, Caer Euni, lying at the end of a long steep-sided ridge above the straight and enclosed valley which runs parallel to that of the Dee. The references in place-names in this area to 'Sarn' and 'Sarnau' (usually translated as 'causeway' but often used in connection with Roman roads and ancient trackways) may indicate that Caer Euni overlooked an important route. The location of the fort is also clearly based on its exceptional outlook over a large area and the easily defended position provided by the sheer fall to the valley, and it must have been of some importance in its day since it merited a large extension, a second phase of building.

HICIACIT
INHOCCO
CERIESLA
PIDVM

CHURCHES AND CASTLES

THE very earliest inhabitants seem to have favoured the coast; that is where the majority of neolithic tombs remain. Iron-age forts such as Caer Euni are also rare inland, and commoner on the Llŷn peninsula than in southern Gwynedd. The Romans, for their part, mainly passed through. They were going from Deva to Segontium, from Segontium to Moridunum. They were not that interested in Meirionnydd, Penllyn and Ardudwy. It was not until some centuries after the Romans left that anybody made a lasting impression on the area of inland southern Gwynedd.

During the late sixth century and at the start of the seventh a number of Celtic Christian missionaries came from Ireland to Scotland and down our coast, and wherever they travelled founded churches. They converted others, who spread their work; and in many cases we know the names of these, such as Beuno, a man of mid Wales who worked both in Powys and on the western seabord of Gwynedd. One of the earliest of these 'saints', we may deduce, was the founder of Dolwyddelan, since we do not know his name but rather his origin. 'Dol' means meadow. 'Gwyddelan' is the diminutive of 'Gwyddel', meaning an Irishman. The little Irishman's meadow.

The description has now become a name, and as St Gwyddelan he will be remembered for ever in the dedication of the church he founded. As it happens Gwyddelan's church has moved, for reasons we shall encounter in a later chapter. He founded it on the hill which lies between the present church and the castle, round which the main road loops, a lumpy hill with a smattering of trees, known as Bryn y Bedd.

A number of features of the older church moved with the construction of the new one, in about 1500. This was not of course Gwyddelan's original, which was made of wood and likely to be quite humble. That however was replaced in the early twelvth-century here, as in so many parts of North Wales, by one of stone. From this twelvth-century building comes the impressive Rood-screen. Another feature which predates the present church hangs from the ceiling of its nave. Known as Gwyddelan's bell, it is a wedge-shaped bell of cast bronze in an old Celtic style, which was dug up in 1850 on the site of the original church and so, quite credibly, is the one brought here from Ireland by the little Irishman himself and rung by him on that hill to call the people of the valley to his services.

There are signs of early Christianity too in the neighbouring valley, the other side of the mountain mass known as Ro-wen, the valley of the Machno. Here in the church are preserved five very early Christian

(15) Inscribed stones at Penmachno commemorate very early Christian burials

(16) Dolwyddelan castle

tombstones which were found in its churchyard. One, in fact, may date from before the end of the fifth century. Another, since its inscription refers to a consul by name, can be dated with some confidence to the year 540. Another has the 'Chi-Rho' symbol, an early Christian code formed from the first two letters of the Greek word for Christ. This stone also refers to its subject as lying 'in hoc congeries lapidum', in this pile of stones, a remarkable indication that the Bronze Age custom of cairn burial had not died out in North Wales in post-Roman times (15).

The next valley beyond that is that of the upper Conwy, and here too by the Middle Ages a surprising religious institution had been set up. Towards the end of the 1180's land near the village called for this reason Ysbyty Ifan was given to the Knights Hospitallers of St John, who set up there a hospice dedicated to St John the Baptist. This provided hospitality, and also enjoyed the right of sanctuary; we shall see in a later chapter the results of the misuse of the latter right.

The only explanation for the setting up and subsequent success of this enterprise is that this was one of the routes taken by pilgrims to the holy island of Bardsey. Up the upper Conwy valley to rise past Ysbyty to the moors, dropping down to the Ffestiniog valley to approach the Llŷn along its southern coast, this would form an alternative route to the one punctuated by great churches along its northern coast.

At that time Llywelyn the Great ruled much of Wales, and under his patronage the hospice's territory was enlarged to include much of the upper Conwy valley. Traditionally Llywelyn is said to have been born at Dolwyddelan, but if this is true it is unlikely to have been in the present castle. He was born in the 1170's, and the earliest parts of the castle seem to belong to the early decades of the next century. Across the road below the castle, however, is a natural hillock, now tree-topped, on which an earlier castle stood. It is possible that this one was the North Wales home of Llywelyn's father, Iorwerth (16).

It is in fact likely that the first version of the present castle was built by Llywelyn himself. Its firmly rectangular tower marks it as early work, before Llywelyn developed the new fashion for d-shaped and finally round keeps.

It is clear that in fact he mixed the two styles, during his period of castle-building. At Cricieth there is a rectangular tower of the same size as that at Dolwyddelan, and at Castell y Bere, south of Dolgellau, which Llywelyn built after his seizing of Meirionnydd from his son Gruffudd in 1221, there are examples of all three forms, the rectangular keep in the middle being

(17) Castell y Bere

(17) Castell y Bere's massive walls give it an air of sound construction

again the same size as that at Dolwyddelan.

It is Dolwyddelan's purity of style that marks it as being early. Llywelyn's keep was in fact even simpler than the romantic fortress which we see now. It was only two storeys high, the top section, with its battlements, being a Victorian edition, the work of Lord Willoughby de Eresby in the late 1840's. Edward I crucially captured Dolwyddelan in the January of 1283, which enabled him to control the Conwy valley and as a result to build his fortress at its crossing at Conwy. At that time he may have raised the tower by another floor. In general he seems to have made the castle more spacious, and the west tower, which is evidently added, being placed against the curtain wall, was probably his work, perhaps replacing an older structure. The dressed stone facing its window and also used in the doorway appears to be Cheshire sandstone, similar to that used by Edward at Conwy. Although its origins are not certain it seems likely that this tower is the 'camera' referred to in Edward's accounts for 1283, from which at least we know that work was done at Dolwyddelan immediately after its capture by the English.

Indeed, from Edward's point of view it formed something of a crucial link complerting the great chain of castles thrown round the heartland of Gwynedd, controlling the route from valley to coast and hence relating both to Conwy and to Cricieth and Harlech the other way.

The presence of the earlier castle on its knoll provided evidence that this route was always worth controlling. The fact that the Roman road crosses the valley at right-angles means that a junction of communications took place here at an early date, and the motte of an early castle at the side of the Roman road deep up the narrow valley of Penamnen indicates that the Roman route remained in use into Norman times.

While Edward was improving the castle at Dolwyddelan the war was not quite over.

Llywelyn ap Gruffudd, grandson of Llywelyn the Great, was killed near Builth Wells in December the previous year, but his brother Dafydd succeeded him. With Edward now controlling Snowdonia he moved south, to the great fortress of Castell y Bere, overlooking the Dysyni valley. Over three thousand men camped in the valley below to besiege it and not surprisingly the garrison in due course surrendered, on April 25th, 1283. Dafydd evaded capture and fled to the mountains, surviving remarkably (in spite of being hunted by seven thousand troops) until June.

Castell y Bere lies in a remote valley off a complex of remote valleys, approached by winding lanes from the isolated village of Abergynolwyn, as

(18) The elegant ruins of Cymer Abbey stand beside the river Mawddach

far from the modern world in context and surroundings as it is possible, in this small country, to get. Hence one can look out from it at the valley and see much what Llywelyn would have seen. Built on a rocky outcrop rising from the valley's floor, it faces all directions, giving views of the whole broad cupped valley lying in its enclosure of surrounding hills (17).

You cannot help being impressed by the massiveness and grandeur of Castell y Bere, the complexity with which it fills its hill and the thickness of the masonry of its outer walls. It gives, even in ruin, an impression of having been well built. Its broad stairways rising now to nowhere give definite hints of magnificence. To add to the intense Welshness of the context the slopes around it are clothed now with moss-covered oaks.

Llywelyn the Great's interest in this area was not restricted to the building of this major seat. Some time before that he had encouraged the foundation of a major Cistercian abbey, that of Cymer, the ruins of which lie in a still tranquil setting hard by the murmuring river Mawddach. The Cistercians favoured locations remote from other settlements, which this remarkably remains. Destroyed at the Dissolution, not much survives of what was evidently quite a large complex; yet the substantial arches of the ruin and the elegant tall lancet windows in one remaining wall gives clues of a degree of splendour (18).

HARLECH

EDWARD and Llywelyn had started their conflict in the border country in 1277, and the tension between them reached a climax when the Welsh prince and his brother led raids on the Marches in the spring of 1282, thus breaking the rather fragile agreement which had been contrived between the two countries. Llywelyn died in a skirmish in mid-Wales at the end of that year, and Edward took advantage of the temporary confusion to launch an all-out invasion of Gwynedd, the heartland and refuge of the independent princes. He threw round the inner sanctuary of Snowdonia a great chain of castles.

The southernmost of these is Harlech (3, 19).

Since we had cause to mention the site of Harlech castle in connection with the mythology, it is possible that this notably prominent rock was a sacred or defensive position before Edward came; but it must be said that there is no evidence of this. Harlech as we have it was one of the castles designed for Edward from scratch by Master James of St George, a Frenchman who had supervised the building of castles in Edward's other territories, and who accompanied him into Wales as master of his works there.

That Master James was a genius in his own field is clearly evident to us today. Each of Edward's North Wales castles bears its own unique style and character; yet each conforms to a rigid overall form demanded by its serious military function. Each one bears touches of symmetry and harmony, and even overt decoration, which makes it individually beautiful. Yet they all worked effectively as formidable tools of war. They are variations on a grandiose theme.

Harlech is undoubtedly the most intimate and domestic of the main three. Caernarfon is palatial and grand, Conwy somewhat intimidating in its aspect of power. Harlech is impressive from the outside, due to its splendid eminence, but in its interior it is the sort of place where one feels one could comfortably live. The great windows of its inner face look onto a securely enclosed court, giving rather the feel of a fortified manor, an atmosphere which comes as all the more of a surprise after the view of it rearing against the sky as one approaches.

Edward sited his castles with the eye of a strategist, a day's march apart and in such positions as could be supplied by sea, from his headquarters at Chester, if land communications were cut off. In view of this it is important to remember, at Harlech, that the coastline has changed, this time the land gaining from the sea. Indeed as one stands on the edge of the outer ward it is

(19) Harlech Castle

(19) The interior of the castle still seems like a dwelling

surprising that so much change could happen in the relatively short period of seven hundred years. This is thought to be partly due to the change of course of the river Dwyryd, which now meets the sea in a combined estuary with the Glaslyn some four miles further north. If the outflow of that river at that time skirted the foot of the castle rock, then Edward's harbour might well have been on that, rather than on the seashore. Certainly the Water-Gate, and the path to the castle known as 'the way from the sea' emphasise, even today, Harlech's maritime role.

Although Harlech was built at the same time as Conwy and Caernarfon, we can see a development in style taking place which was to lead, a few years later, to the fully concentric form of Beaumaris. Harlech is in a transitional position between the older form of inner and outer wards, (developed from the keep and bailey fortresses of the earlier Middle Ages), on the one hand, in which the inner citadel is approached through the outer, and on the other the doubling-up effect displayed at Beaumaris, in which the outer ward completely encircles the inner. One can see Master James approaching this later idea at Harlech.

Once there, the castle attracted its own history. It was finished in about 1290, and immediately tested in the revolt of Madog ap Llywelyn in 1294-5. Although besieged by land, it proved the effectiveness of its water-based position, and the garrison held out against the rebels by receiving supplies by sea. Cricieth castle, refortified by Edward, proved equally effective in his service.

For a time there was peace, the system set up by Edward effectively ruling Wales. The death of Richard II in 1399 and the usurpation of the throne by Henry IV, however, led to a less settled situation. It was due to a dispute with a neighbour that Owain Glyndŵr found himself out of favour with the new king, and forced into the role of rebel. But evidently the time was ripe for rebellion, and all that had been lacking was a leader.

In 1401 Glyndŵr failed to take the king's castles of Caernarfon and Harlech, but he tried again in the case of Harlech in 1404. By now he had an unexpected advantage, as the garrison there had become mutinous, weakened by illness, and had started to desert. Glyndŵr seized his chance, negotiated with the pitiful remnant in the castle, and eventually bribed them with cash into surrender.

It was a chance which for a time radically affected his campaign, since he now had a headquarters. He moved his family into the pleasantly habitable security of Harlech – his wife, daughter and son-in-law, Sir Edmund

Mortimer, with his four grandchildren – and for four years it was his home and capital. There, in the tradition of his ancestors at their courts, he called his Council and appointed officers.

The dream did not last. Glyndŵr could not sustain for long enough the backing of his countrymen, and when things began to look less hopeful they deserted him. In 1408 the prince and his family found themselves besieged in Harlech by a force of a thousand men. Harlech castle suffered some of the damage which it bears today in a long bombardment. Mortimer, his son-in-law, had died in the meantime, but his wife and daughter were taken prisoner. In the manner of folk heroes he himself, however, simply disappeared. He was thought to have lived for some time, outlawed and in disguise, and the date and manner of his death is still unknown.

Glyndŵr's biography and personality are essentially larger than life, and stories of a distinctly folktale nature clustered around him. Once, for instance, when he was staying with the Vaughan family in this area – an ancient line of landowners who had seats at Cors y Gedol, south of Harlech, and Nannau near Dolgellau – he was shot by his host at point-blank range. The arrow bounced off, and the attempted assassination rebounded on the hapless Vaughan, who was thought to have been immured in a hollow oak.

Harlech became prominent again in Britain's next internal struggle, the long-drawn-out Wars of the Roses, when it was a Lancastrian stronghold, and indeed held out against the victorious Yorkists longer than any other fortress. It is to this period of siege and resistance that its famous song belongs, the tune of which is traditional and finds echoes in the anthems of other nations.

Medieval castles were the most sophisticated weapon of their time, but could not anticipate the innovations of later centuries, and their usefulness effectively ceased with the development of artillery. The power of gunpowder enabled the projecting of missiles over their high walls in constant bombardment, and the battering they received in these later times has left many of them in a much more ruined state than Harlech. In the Civil War of the 17th century Harlech castle was defended for the King and besieged by Oliver Cromwell's brother-in-law, a local landowner called Colonel John Jones, who later came to be one of the signatories to the King's death-warrant. His ancestral home, Maes y Garnedd, may be seen at the very end of the lane which runs up the narrow Nantcol valley.

Harlech castle withstood the siege of Colonel Jones, but eventually it surrendered to the Parliamentary army under General Mytton, in 1647. Just as it had been the last of the Lancastrian castles in Britain to fall to the Yorkists, so it was the last castle to hold out for the King against Parliament, and the Civil War was over with its surrender. That event proved to be its last military act, and from then on it has been an unoccupied ruin.

You would not think that such a quiet place could have been involved in so much history. Harlech today has few notable buildings, and indeed it seems that it never had. Pennant, in the late 18th century, describes it as being "a small and very poor town, remarkable only for its castle". Speed's map of 1610 shows only a scattering of cottages some distance from the castle. It seems that Edward I did not establish there the borough which provided a garrison of English families to administer this government, as he did at Conwy and Caernarfon. Perhaps the reason is that he had created a borough already at Cricieth nearby, to which he may have hoped to entice the essential English colony to control this area.

The town which survives under the shadow of the castle now is pleasant and successful, still small enough to have an intimate and friendly atmosphere.

NDS
BARCLAYS

GLYNDŴR AND THE AFTERMATH

DOLGELLAU is a mellow market town today, its solid stone appearance testifying to centuries of relative affluence, based during the eighteenth and nineteenth centuries on the weaving of wool, milled by water-power, and heightened in the mid-nineteenth century by a period of mineral exploitation. One is not at all surprised to hear that it was visited by all the great travelling writers, by Leland, Camden, Pennant and even Wordsworth (20).

It was from here, in the year 1404, that a remarkable document was sent from 'Owynus dei gratia princeps Wallie' to the king of France. This is the main evidence we have that Dolgellau was the site of one of Owain's parliaments. It is known that his main parliament was held at Machynlleth, further south, and no doubt his council was also summoned to his headquarters at Harlech. But that he wrote to Charles VI explicitly from Dolgellau, on 10th May, 1404, means that this sturdy brown town was, at least for a time, at the forefront of national events.

The letter is significant for a number of reasons, not least that it forms the first time Owain has formally called himself Prince of Wales. It shows too the precarious position of the English crown, since the French were only too ready to side with the rebels. Owain asked for arms and assistance and was at once promised them. The French did in fact send a fleet, and although things did not quite work out as expected there was a moment when Wales was an international power.

Owain's main activities, and the bitter conclusion of his campaign affected Harlech, and Cricieth too (as we have seen) did not go unscathed. Sir John Wynn, writing at the end of the sixteenth century, attributes the desolate state of much of North Wales, particularly the upper reaches of the Conwy valley, to depopulation caused by Owain's scorched-earth policy:

> All the whole country then was but a forest, rough and spacious as it is still, but then waste of inhabitants and all overgrown with woods, for Owain Glyndŵr's wars, beginning in Anno 1400, continued fifteen years, which brought such a desolation . . . for it was Owain Glyndŵr's policy to bring all things to waste, that the English should find not strength nor resting-place in the country.

(20) Dolgellau

(21) The ruins of Maredudd's homestead stand beside the Roman road in Cwm Penamnen

(22) The 'Dolwyddelan dragon', supposedly the water-monster to blame for the Conwy valley floods

No doubt other factors, such as plague and disorder during the intervening period of the Wars of the Roses, were to blame as well. It is interesting to hear, however, that for one reason or another the moorland country around Penmachno and Dolwyddelan was a wasteland when, round about 1485, Sir John's great-grandfather moved his family up from Eifionydd to occupy Dolwyddelan castle.

By then the castle was only partly inhabitable, though it had apparently remained occupied, since the previous occupant was a well-known outlaw. Maredudd ap Ieuan (as this ancestor of the Wynn family is known) needed the security of Dolwyddelan's walls, since the whole area was infested with bandits. He had left Eifionydd because of the fierceness of family feuds, saying he had rather fight with outlaws and thieves than with his own kinsmen, 'for if I live in my own house in Eifionydd I must either kill my own kinsmen or be killed by them'. Up here at Dolwyddelan however there was a different problem.

The hospice of St John at Ysbyty Ifan had, as we have remarked, the right of sanctuary, being run by knights under their own rules. Over the centuries this had developed into a curious inversion of its intended protection, and become the haven of outlaws and thieves. "No place within twenty miles about," says Sir John, "was safe from their incursions and robbery."

In due course the castle became too small for Maredudd's expanding family. That would perhaps be surprising were it not for his unusual fecundity. He had ten children by his first wife, two by his second, and three by a third woman. There were also at least six others by less stable relationships. After living in the castle for some years he built himself a large house in Cwm Penamnen, a narrow steep-sided valley south of the town, through which runs the Roman road, Sarn Helen.

When Maredudd moved to Cwm Penamnen (where ruins of his homestead may be seen beside the road, deep in the private world of the cwm) he also moved St Gwyddelan's church (21). The reason was, Sir John discovered from his uncles, that the old church stood in a thicket, where he might too easily be ambushed. The whole of this story is puzzling. It would, first, have been easier to cut down the thicket. Secondly the present church is surrounded by immense and ancient yews, one of which is sometimes said to be three thousand years old. This would seem to indicate that the church has always been where it now is, located, as almost all old Welsh churches are, on the site of a heathen religious monument. Yet this is not the case; it is certain that about 1500 Maredudd had the original church on Bryn y Bedd

(23) The memorial to Maredudd and his wife in Dolwyddelan church

demolished and this one built.

One reason he might have done so is that from the south-east window you can see the top of Y Garreg Big, and from there you can see (or could before the trees were planted) his homestead in Cwm Penamnen:

> Certain it was that he dared not go to church on a Sunday from his house of Penamnen but that he must have the same guarded with men and have the doors sure barred and bolted and a watchman to stand at Y Garreg Big during divine service (being a rock whence he might see both the church and the house and raise the cry if the house were assaulted).

Although the present south-east window is in the south chapel, which is a sixteenth century addition, its predecessor in Maredudd's original building might well have allowed him to see his lookout from his pew.

The church is a charming building with a staunch air of age, a firm beam structure raising its roof with some impressive wooden vaulting at the chancel end. Of special interest is the 'Dolwyddelan dragon', a figure carved on a wooden lintel in low relief, depicting a strange snake-like creature with folded wings, a long neck at one end knotted in the middle and a head at both ends, one of which has an extended tongue. Challenged to think up a thing that no-one has ever seen, you could do worse than come up with the Dolwyddelan dragon. The carving came from a demolished church further down the valley, and is thought to represent the Conwy valley water-monster, the 'afanc', which lived in Beaver Pool at Betws-y-coed, from where it caused the familiar Conwy valley floods, until it was dragged by oxen over the hills and deposited in a mountain lake. A mistaken exercise, as it turned out: it was not the monster, evidently, which was causing the floods, since they still go on (22).

The other special feature of the church, and one which alone would justify a visit, is the brass memorial to Maredudd himself. This diminutive portrait shows, in a simple style but with a very high degree of skilled craftsmanship, a man at prayer though in full armour, which we may gather was Maredudd's enforced custom. His eyes are alert, perhaps fixed on the watchman on the rock beyond the south-east window (23).

In ornate Gothic lettering in Latin underneath we are admonished to

> Pray for the souls of Meredith ap Ivan ap Robt Esq and Alice his wife who died the 18th day of March 1525 on whose souls God have mercy. Amen.

(24) Tŷ Mawr Wybrnant, birthplace of Bishop Morgan, who translated the Bible into Welsh

GLYNDŴR AND THE AFTERMATH

There are reminders everywhere in this area of its old traditional connection with religion. At the back of nowhere, between the Lledr and the Machno valleys, is another place of pilgrimage. Tŷ Mawr Wybrnant is a solidly built old house set in its own valley in the hills, lovingly restored and maintained by the National Trust. Its eminent importance in Welsh culture is due to the fact that it was the birthplace, in 1545, of William Morgan, who became Bishop of St Asaph at the time when Sir John Wynne, Maredudd's descendant, was presiding over his great estates at Gwydir, in the Conwy valley. Bishop Morgan has the distinction of being the first translator of the complete Bible into Welsh, and Tŷ Mawr now houses a fine collection of early Welsh Bibles in memory of this (24).

SLATE AND RAILWAYS

THE rivers Glaslyn and Dwyryd converge at the bottom of the Ffestiniog valley, and their emergence in the delta country of Traeth Mawr forms a convenient boundary between the north-west and the southern parts of the new county of Gwynedd. Consequently the reclamation of Traeth Mawr and the formation of the port of Porthmadog are described in the companion booklet to this, *Llŷn, the Peninsula's story*. The rise of the slate industry concerns us here as well. It happened that the vast dome of Silurian rock which closes the head of the Ffestiniog valley, in which the Cynfal merges with the Dwyryd, contains material ideal for making roofing-slates.

One of the effects of increasing industrialism was a shift in population, away from the land and into urban complexes. This had already got under way before the end of the eighteenth century, and at the turn of the century and in the early nineteenth it was happening all over Europe. Thus (as is mentioned in the other booklet) the price of slates doubled between 1798 and 1825. It is a significant fact for North Wales. It gave rise, among other things, to Blaenau Ffestiniog (25).

The quarries there were in operation before the end of the century, but it took the entrepreneurial and administrative skills of one forceful man, the young (as he was then) Samuel Holland, who arrived in 1821 to sort out his father's business, to spot and seize the providential opportunity. In just four years he had built there a major business.

Progress feeds on itself. Holland could not have got his quarry's 10,000 tons a year of slates out from Blaenau and around the world if he had continued the age-old means of transport. On the backs of pack animals to the valley floor, then in carts down to the Dwyryd, by small boat down the shallow river to load the beached schooners on the tidal sandbanks, the slates made their painstaking progress. Holland changed all that.

Railways were not new, when Samuel Holland, having acquired a quay in the new harbour of Porthmadog, succeeded in getting a railway bill through Parliament, against local opposition, in 1833. Quarries had used wagonways since the sixteenth century. They were not even new in North Wales, since Lord Penrhyn had a five mile track built between 1800 and 1801 to connect his quarry to the port called by the same name, Port Penrhyn. A railway ran from Caernarfon to the slate quarries at Nantlle from 1824-5, which also took copper ore from Drws-y-coed. What was new about this particular railway was that, right from the start, it carried passengers.

These early railways were powered by horses and by gravity, and

(25) Slate workings at Blaenau Ffestiniog

(25) Old quarrymen's barracks at Cwmorthin, Blaenau Ffestiniog

Holland's, to start with, was no exception. "All went up," he himself wrote, "to the inclines in carriages drawn by horses, but we all came down without horses, the inclination being sufficient to enable us to do so." The horses came down in the train as well, "feeding all the way".

That was in 1838, and it made the Ffestiniog railway the first public light railway in the world. It is notable too for its narrow gauge, which Holland was advised would be cheaper to construct and "less to pay for the land taken". This characteristic proved influential, and experiments here in the 1860's led to the adoption of a similar form in light railways elsewhere in Britain and in North America.

In the meantime another innovation was taking place. Steam power replaced horses in many places from the 1830's, and in 1863 it reached the Ffestiniog valley. At first it was thought that the narrow track and the sharp curves would make this impossible, but Holland had a nephew as enterprising as himself who drew up his own design.

Remarkably this pioneering line is still in operation, in fact forming one of North Wales major visitor attractions. In 1996 it carried 327,000 people. Its industrial purpose has of course given way to the exploitation of North Wales' major asset, its unrivalled scenery. Now conveniently joining up at Blaenau Ffestiniog with the branch line up the Conwy valley (itself started in the 1860's) it offers a railway experience which it would be hard to match (26).

It was in fact partly the further development of the Conwy valley line in the 1870's that led to the decline of the Ffestiniog line. Another railway also reached Blaenau Ffestiniog from Bala, and down in the valley of the Dwyryd the use of the port of Porthmadog was itself challenged by the construction of the Cambrian Coast Line, which could take slates from Minffordd southwards to link up with the growing network. Patterns of communication were changing, and so, during the first decades of this century, were types of roofing material. By the 1920's the Ffestiniog narrow-gauge was largely a tourist attraction, and during the war it closed to passengers. In August 1946 it closed completely, and lay abandoned. Work started on restoration in 1954, and by 1982 the complete line was rehabilitated. It remains largely staffed by volunteers.

If the Ffestiniog narrow-gauge has changed its nature, from conveying 130,000 tons of slate a year at its peak to its current score of 327,000 passengers, Porthmadog's other light railway was designed to carry tourists from the start. The Welsh Highland Railway, built in the 1920's was in

(26) *The Ffestiniog narrow-gauge railway*

effect a link between the Ffestiniog narrow-gauge and yet another stretch of line, formerly called the North Wales Narrow Gauge Railway, which crossed to the coast south of Caernarfon. This was never the success it was expected to be, and in due course it closed and became a footpath until the renewed interest in light railways led to the formation of a company to reopen it, at the end of the 1990's.

Railways are not the only legacy left to tourism by slate. Blaenau Ffestiniog now has a declining population and lack of industrial base, but it boasts two major tourist attractions, the Llechwedd slate caverns and the Gloddfa Ganol slate mine and quarry. These provide views of the old workings and an insight into the history of the industry.

While Blaenau Ffestiniog remains linked to the world by railway, and so will continue to provide facilities (which can be coupled with train rides) such as the slate museums, for a long time its neighbouring town of Bala remained linked by rail as well. Here, however, the major effects of the slate industry were missing, and a strongly contrasting rural Welsh world has persisted.

BALA

BALA's oldest structure, 'Tomen Bala', has in the past excited curiosity, but today unfortunately invites rather the reverse (27). Hidden by houses and covered in bushes and trees, it is not quite the prominence which it no doubt once was. In Pennant's day its slopes were covered with townspeople knitting, since that was the main industry of the town, and from its top there was a fine view of the lake and the surrounding hills. When George Borrow came, some hundred years later, it was still impressive, described by him as one of "that brotherhood of artificial mounds of unknown antiquity, found scattered, here and there, throughout Europe and the greater part of Asia". While Pennant says it was probably Roman, and the site of a small fort, Borrow inclines to think that before its use as a stronghold, or alternatively a temple, it was a burial mound.

In fact it is probably nothing more exciting than a medieval motte, a form very common in some areas of Wales and the Midlands, represented in these parts by the mound up at the Roman camp of Tomen y Mur and another, known as Glyndŵr's Mount, also alongside the river Dee near Carrog . These mottes formed the keep section of motte and bailey castles put up, often quite quickly and temporarily, by Norman Marcher lords, a style of military defence connected with the feudal system and the Norman invasion and very common during the twelfth century.

Of course there remains the possibility that whoever constructed the mound at Bala, whther or not a medieval motte, may have made use of an artificial mound of more ancient date. It is known that the vast burial mounds of Ireland were used at later times as defensive positions, and no doubt the feudal lords in building their castles used whatever existing natural or artificial assistance lay to hand.

Who may have fortified medieval Bala is not known, nor is much known about its history in subsequent centuries. It features in the charters of the Welsh princes – Llywelyn the Great is said to have founded a castle there in 1202 – and in connection with the castle at Harlech in the 14th century, so it was almost certainly fortified by alternate sides in the Plantagenet wars of invasion.

By the time Pennant wrote about his journey, in the 18th century, Bala was a thriving producer of woollen goods and a busy market centre for them. Everyone in the town, in his description, was engaged in knitting stockings. The wool, he tells us, came from the Conwy valley market. He noted the regular appearance of Bala's town plan, which made him wonder if

(27) 'Tomen Bala', probably the mound of a motte-and-bailey castle, is now obscured by shrubs and surrounded by buildings.

(28) Statue of Thomas Charles in Bala's Tegid Street

(29) The statue of Tom Ellis, the influential 19th century Liberal M.P., dominates Bala's main street

it had Roman origins. The name, he says, comes from the word for a river flowing out of a lake.

By George Borrow's time, the mid-19th century, not much had changed. It was a sizeable town then – he estimates three to four thousand as its population – but with the same simple street plan as today. Borrow stayed at the White Lion, where he was impressed by the breakfast. He notes the fervent interest in religion which is one of Bala's chief distinctions, recording the spirited resistance which was made in Bala at that time by the Anglican church against the general upsurge of Methodism.

Bala's flowering came (and went) with the Methodist Revival. The town's connection with this seems to start with an episode in 1800, when a girl called Mary Jones walked thirty miles across the hills barefoot to acquire a bible. The great Thomas Charles of Bala, to whom she came, was obliged to give her his own, and so struck was he by this inequity of demand and supply that he was inspired to found the British and Foreign Bible Society. More influentially even than this, Charles founded the Sunday School movement, to which Welsh rural education owes so much, and also the Welsh Calvinistic Methodist body. It was perhaps his act of personally ordaining the latter's first eight ministers which forms the moment of that powerful movement's birth, in Bala, in 1811. A statue of Charles now stands in Tegid Street (28).

Subsequently Bala became prominent as the centre for the training of Calvinist Methodist ministers. The former college, now the offices of the Welsh Presbyterian Youth Chaplain, is one of Bala's several religious buildings.

Other notable figures in Welsh cultural and social history abound in Bala. Tom Ellis, Member of Parliament for Meirionnydd in the second half of the 19th century, was the inspiration for the radical wing of the Liberal Party, again a movement very much attuned to Welsh attitudes. His statue occupies a more prominent spot than Charles', in the town's main street (29). The survival of the Welsh language through a time of severe suppresion owes much to a Bala father and son, Sir Owen M. Edwards, founder of *Cymru*, and Sir Ifan ab Owen Edwards who continued his good work on behalf of Welsh language and culture in the early part of this century.

Another remarkable piece of Welsh history originates from Bala. In 1865 the Reverend Michael D. Jones (30), principal of Bala's College of Congregationalists, fitted out a sailing ship, the *Mimosa*, which took 153 men, women and children to Pagatonia in South America, in order that they

(30) Michael D. Jones of Bala, 1822-1898

(31) Bala's narrow-gauge railway

might be able to practise unpersecuted their non-conformist religion, and their language. The result is that there is still in Patagonia a Welsh-speaking colony, one of history's more improbable sagas of heroism and determination and one of its more curious survivals.

Remarkably another now world-famous tradition, the sheep-dog trial, also arose in Bala, the first being held outside the town in 1873.

From all this it will be seen that Bala is quintessentially Welsh. Now no longer linked to the world by railway, and never on any major road route, it has a feeling of remoteness and independence accentuated by one's probable approach over moorland or by winding lane through rolling fields. It is a compact town surrounded by miles of empty upland country.

From this very sound background Bala is now emerging into a new era, that of the booming leisure industry. Possessing as it does the largest inland area of natural water in Wales, it has the assets required to make a visitor's journey worthwhile. Traditionally its vast surrounding moorland made it the centre of the autumn sport of grouse shooting. Now its 1,084 acres of water are helping it to thrive as a site of summertime recreation as well.

Llyn Tegid now offers fishing, sailing, skin-diving and bird-watching, the large variety of wild life retained by an enlightened ban on power boats of all kinds. Among other water birds there are said to be six species of duck, and the herons and cormorants are no doubt gratified by the fourteen species of fish which swim in the lake's brown waters. One, which has survived from the ice age by living at a depth too great for rod or beak, is unique to Llyn Tegid, and unique also in only having a name in Welsh, the Gwyniad.

Even Bala's defunct railway (axed by Beeching in the 1960's) has been reincarnated as a narrow-gauge line, on the original route, which has run along the south shore of the lake since 1972 (31).

Mountain scenery, wool, non-conformism, Sunday schools, sheep-dog trials, the defence of the ancient language, narrow-gauge railways and recreation. It is as if Bala has been chosen to be the representative of all that is most distinctive about North Wales.

MODERN TIMES

THE same upland dome which the Dee and its headwaters drains in the Bala direction is drained as well by the Mawddach running the other way. This runs down through Coed y Brenin, a vast wooded area which possesses some of Wales' famous gold, to become estuarial where it meets the Wnion below Dolgellau. Here at Bontddu there is again a tradition of gold mining. The valley opens then to reveal an asset which has turned out to be even more valuable. Classic North Wales scenery, endlessly appealing in its blend of subtlety and grandeur (32).

Ruskin famously said that in the whole of Britain there was only one walk more beautiful than than from Barmouth to Dolgellau, and that was the walk from Dolgellau to Barmouth. The poet G.M. Hopkins passed this way too, and wrote a poem about Penmaen Pool, 'for the Visitor's Book at the Inn'. None of this high romanticism is an appropriate preparation for the rather prosaic reality of Barmouth, at the estuary's outlet.

It is surprising to what extent the towns of southern Gwynedd have grown to be distinct in character. Barmouth adds to this the further distinction of being several different types of town in one. Its name, even, is a hybrid, since it does not mean, as it seems, that this is the mouth of the Bar. Rather this is an English confusion about the Welsh name Aber Maw, the mouth of the Mawddach, again contracted in local Welsh to 'Bermo' (33).

While the present Barmouth is part seaside resort, part fishing port, and in physical terms dates largely from the second half of the last century, its origins are apparently very much older, since tradition maintains that the old house on the quay, 'Tŷ Gwyn yn Bermo', was originally built by the Vaughans of Cors y Gedol for the young Henry Tudor. The old town, which crawls in winding alleyways up the crags, along with the neighbouring scenery, attracted Victorian romantics and academics, and Barmouth was visited by Tennyson, Wordsworth, Shelley, Ruskin and Darwin.

It was perhaps Ruskin whose presence here became the most influential. The headland above the old town, and a number of properties in the area, belonged at the time to a Mrs Talbot, who was a friend of his. Because of his interest in social reform she donated some of the old cottages on the rock to form the basis of a trust, with which Ruskin set up the Guild of St George's, an early experiment in subsided housing and rent control. Further Mrs Talbot, with Ruskin's encouragement, actually founded here the National Trust, by giving it, in 1895, its first property, the top of the craggy headland above the old town, "to be kept and guarded for the enjoyment of Barmouth for ever".

(32) Bridge over River Mawddach at Penmaenpool

(33) Barmouth

MODERN TIMES

Undoubtedly the greatest change in this largely idyllic area was the coming of the railway, linking Barmouth to Tywyn and hence to Mid Wales. The Cambrian Coast Line would not have been possible without Barmouth bridge, a half-mile viaduct across the estuary, opened in 1860. A footpath runs alongside the railway, out over the great sheet of tidal water, giving a superb view of the river stretching inland and the looming beauty of Cader Idris rearing above it.

Ardudwy, in fact, is neatly bounded by two great estuaries; and moving north again and further into modern times we find the combined effects of the emergence of the Glaslyn and the Dwyryd giving rise to a highly-favoured headland which has been put to a rather surprising use.

Portmeirion, like so much we have considered in this area, is the result of the determination and creativity of a single forceful individual (34). The late Sir Clough Williams-Ellis acquired an overgrown headland and started to clear its undergrowth in 1926, having identified its mild climate and secluded position as being the perfect situation for his romantic vision of an ideal village. The land had previously belonged to his uncle, once the site of a small settlement and landscaped with tree-planting and rhododendrons during the mid-19th century.

Sir Clough (who died in 1978 at the age of 94) was a largely self-trained architect, the descendant of Caernarfonshire landowners, who became fashionable and successful in London in the 1920's. His work may be seen in various parts of the country and the world, but particularly in his home area, where his liking for urns and pedestals has left his distinctive mark on the gateways and grounds of many country houses. He it was who designed the grave of Lloyd George at Llanystumdwy, bringing together two of the powerful personalities of this area. A man very much in the mould of Madocks, he is rightly described in *The Times*'s obituary as "his own best work".

Having first converted the old house by the sea to a hotel, Williams-Ellis began to collect from various parts of the country interesting and rare buildings, which he had dismantled, transported and re-erected at Portmeirion. The result is a fanciful and amusing world, a total environment intended only to please.

This extraordinary project developed over a span of more than thirty years, the last item (the Colonnade, a structure formerly in Bristol) being added in 1959. Portmeirion has had its times of fame and fashion, most recently when it became nationally known as the location of the television

(34) Portmeirion

(35) Trawsfynydd

series, 'The Prisoner'. In the pre-war years it was a favourite retreat of the Duke of Windsor, and Noel Coward wrote his play 'Blithe Spirit' there, up in the Watch House, during a single week.

The unexpected is a frequent occurrence in this area as a whole, where a great range of historic land uses is packed into a relatively small mileage. Perhaps this is most striking where it is most directly related to our modern age, as at the nuclear power station which overlooks the lake at Trawsfynydd (35).

Now decommissioned, Trawsfynydd power station still presents problems for the future, since there is no easy or safe way of removing and disposing of radioactive material. At a continuing cost, and for an inevitably protracted period, its looming presence squats over the lake as a reminder of the uncertainties of modern science.

Such issues are perhaps not typical of this largely idyllic area, but they are in scale with its strong character and its constant ability to surprise. Indeed to stand on Tomen y Mur, amid the remains of a Roman fort and among the associations of old mythology, and to see on the one hand moorland unchanged since the wizard Gwydion came there, whenever that might have been, and on the other the embodiment of our present uneasy and dangerous times, is to receive a significant shock. This is a land where history is built into the terrain, and it still goes on.